Adira,

You are truly a

~Gift~

to so many people,

including me !!

Wishing only the best

for you forever &

Always!

XOXO

Yolander Spears

4/26/2021

The Gift

Yolande Nicholson Spears

June 2012

INFINITY
PUBLISHING

Copyright © 2012 by Yolande Nicholson Spears

ISBN 978-0-7414-6765-2 Paperback
ISBN 978-0-7414-7394-3 Hardcover
ISBN 978-0-7414-9539-6 eBook

Printed in the United States of America

Published June 2012

INFINITY PUBLISHING
1094 New DeHaven Street, Suite 100
West Conshohocken, PA 19428-2713
Toll-free (877) BUY BOOK
Local Phone (610) 941-9999
Fax (610) 941-9959
Info@buybooksontheweb.com
www.buybooksontheweb.com

Preface

The story you're about to read takes place between 1957 and 1964. In a series of vignettes, chronicled in a young girl's voice, it details events that took place in my life between the ages of seven and fourteen. And while I've taken some stylistic liberties to better serve the story, the experiences described—whether rooted in physical fact or emotional reality —are true.

Many things prompted the writing of this narrative. First and foremost, I wanted to inspire young readers, helping them understand that no matter how overwhelming, challenges can almost always be overcome. I also wanted to champion the cause of art and arts education. I hoped that my story might awaken adults to the transformational role these vital subjects can play in the lives of youth. Finally, I wanted to pay tribute to a host of extraordinary people.

These include my grandfather, a freed slave, whose half-white sister secretly taught him to read in a candlelit barn. This was no small accomplishment. As a slave he could be hung, burned alive, or shot to death for learning to read or count. I also extend my gratitude to my father, a man whose love of reading and poetry inspired my own belief in the power of the word to transform people's lives. And I have the utmost respect for the thousands of educators in schools and in the African-American churches who have dedicated their lives to developing the intellectual, artistic, and spiritual potential of young people.

Above all, I write for my mother—Juliette Williamson Nicholson. Despite a life marred by daunting poverty, health challenges, and heartbreaking upheavals, she managed to instill in me and my siblings the importance of improving our minds, tending our bodies, caring for our communities, and nurturing our souls. Even more, she taught us—through example and loving instruction—to always believe we could fulfill our dreams, no matter how impossible or faraway they might seem.

To her—and all the women like her—I bow down in absolute awe.

***

I felt Mama gently shaking me. I opened my eyes. The room was dark.

"Get dressed," she said. "Don't ask any questions. And please, Yoli, hurry."

As soon as I'd pulled on my clothes, Mama rushed me, my sister and brothers into the backseat of Uncle Sax's Buick.

"Where are we going?" I asked as the car roared into action.

"On a trip, honey."

"Without Daddy?"

Mama hesitated. "Yes. Without Daddy."

I hated to think of Daddy all alone in the apartment. So I patted Mama on the shoulder. When she didn't respond, I clutched her silky hair.

"Stop that! You're going to wake Kevin."

"When Daddy wakes up, is he coming to meet us?"

"No, Daddy's not meeting us. He's got to work."

"Is he coming to meet us after work?"

"No."

"Why not?"

"Because we're going to your Aunt Ada's house in Kentucky. You're going to have a wonderful summer vacation."

"Are you staying with us in Kentucky?"

Mama sighed. "No, Baby, I'm dropping you off at Aunt Ada's and then coming back to St. Louis. While I'm gone, I need you to be a big girl and help Greg take care of Jessica and Kevin. Can you do that for me?"

My stomach tightened as questions raged through my mind: How could I take care of my younger sister and brother without Mama? What if Mama and Daddy started fighting again and she forgets to pick us up?"

My heart pounded. "When are you coming back?"

"I'll be gone just a few months. Now please, Yolande! Let go of me and try to take a nap."

Mama started to sing as she often did to ease us into sleep. I think this was her way of praying. When she reached the second verse of *Jesus Loves Me This I Know,* I put my jacket over my head, hiding my tears. Finally, serenaded by her soft singing, I drifted off.

When I opened my eyes, the car had stopped on the side of the road. Uncle Sax was lifting the potty bucket from the trunk. Mama told everyone to get out and pee. After that, we sat in a circle, munching on bologna sandwiches. Between bites, Uncle Sax cursed a man named Jim Crow.

In earlier visits south, Daddy had cursed Jim Crow too. "People of color should fight against Jim Crow! Or else we should move to England or Canada," he'd shout. Mama always shushed him, though I know she was proud of him for speaking his mind.

After eating we piled back into the car. Mama passed out coloring and comic books. For awhile, I happily drew and read, though soon the car's monotonous motion lulled me to sleep.

But within minutes of drifting off, Uncle Sax's voice startled me awake.

"The children!" he shouted, "Quick, cover them!"

"On the floor!" Mama said as she threw a blanket over us.

"Lord Jesus! The work of demons!" Uncle Sax boomed as he got out of the car. He yelled to Mama to lock the doors.

Frightened, but curious, I lifted the corner of my blanket and peered through the window. I could see Uncle Sax running towards two men struggling to release a charred lump swinging from the branch of a scorched tree. A group of women huddled nearby, holding on to each other, weeping and wailing.

Mama turned around, her face fearful. "Down! Everyone down!"

I dove to the car floor, squeezing my eyes shut. The air settled in my lungs so thick I felt like I was drowning in a swamp.

When the door yanked open, my mouth went dry. Beads of sweat trickled down my temples, burning my eyes. I wanted to scream, but I couldn't find my voice. The monsters were coming to get us.

But it wasn't the monsters. It was Uncle Sax. "We're in Klan country," he said. "We're not stopping 'til we get outta this damn place."

As we drove away, Mama instructed us to get up from the floor. Through the rear window I saw a lump on the ground, its blackened feet sticking out from the blanket's edge.

Terrified, I soiled my pants.

Mama's voice was soft and slow, trying for my sake not to be scared. "It's all right Baby," she soothed. "As soon as we get away from here, we'll pull off the road and change."

After that, we didn't make any more stops though Aunt Ada's house was still a long, long way away.

***

When we finally arrived at Aunt Ada's, she was sitting on her big, white porch, the late afternoon light washing over her apricot colored skin. This was the third time I'd seen Aunt Ada and she was just as pretty as I'd remembered.

Mama hurried up onto the porch, laughing and smiling. After squeezing Mama, Kevin, Jessica, and Greg so hard I feared they'd break, she scooped me up in her arms, her bracelets jingling like tiny glass bells. Aunt Ada then gestured for us to follow her into the house. She led us to a lacy table covered with platters of pineapple glazed ham, collard greens, deviled eggs, fried fish, string beans, and baked macaroni and cheese, my favorite food in the world.

After we'd eaten our meal, we gathered around Aunt Ada's ebony piano. I stretched out across her plush carpet and as she sang to the piano's bright and deep notes, my fears slowly faded.

But when Aunt Ada closed her music book and Mama announced it was time for us all to go to bed, they came racing back. I hated saying goodnight to Mama because I knew she'd be gone in the morning.

As I lay in bed, images looped around in my mind. I saw a scorched tree. Women huddled together. Burned, black feet. Trying to chase away these frightful scenes, I switched on the light and began fervently praying to God, asking him to protect me and Mama and Daddy and Kevin and Jessica and Greg. When that didn't chase my fears away, I began humming Mama's favorite melodies.

Fortunately, as the days passed, those evil memories faded from my mind. Aunt Ada was so sweet and I loved my bedroom, with its canopy bed and plushy carpeting and the living room with its paintings, sculptures, and big black piano. Each night, we'd gather round that piano. I even got to turn pages as Aunt Ada sang and played. Aunt Ada's playing—sometimes fun and fast and other times slow and sweet as Mama's homemade molasses—always made me feel better.

There were other wonderful things too.

Aunt Ada taught me how to recite poetry and put my thoughts and feeling into songs. And every Sunday, we sang in the Youth Choir. I loved everything about that choir but especially how all the separate voices came together into one song—like lots of patches blending into one quilt. I wished I could sing in a choir like this back in St. Louis. But though Mama loved music as much as Aunt Ada, I knew that wasn't going to happen. Daddy was mad at God and thought church-going was silly.

Early one evening, a few weeks into my visit, I asked Aunt Ada why Daddy was so mad at God.

Aunt Ada pursed her lips as she placed a dish in the drain board. "Yolande, your father faced tremendous prejudice. It didn't matter that he'd been a soldier and honored veteran in World War II, an author, and poet. In the end, his talent meant less than the color of his skin."

She went on, describing how Daddy had quit his accounting job when his boss called him 'boy'. "Your Daddy could deal with no promotions and no raises...but being called 'boy'—that was too much. But Jesse Nicholson wasn't a quitter. He was a fighter. And smart. So he took all the money he'd saved and opened up his own appliance business. In the first two years, he made more than $150,000. He was generous too. He sent money to your Aunt Becky so she could finish college. He also helped your Aunt Clara buy a house in Memphis. Sometimes he let people buy on credit when they were short of cash. Because of this, the whole neighborhood looked up to him. Soon things were going so well, he planned to open a second store. But suddenly everything went wrong. Because your Daddy refused to do what the mob said, they burned down his store. After that, he began drinking too much. And that's why your Mother bought you all here. They're trying to work things out. Do you understand?"

At the mention of Daddy's drinking, Aunt Ada's cheerful kitchen began to blur. I threw down my dish towel and dashed out the back door. Flinging myself on the ground near the rose bushes, I sobbed, feeling one of the deepest sorrows I'd ever felt. I tried to calm myself, but it was no use. No sooner did I stop crying then the tears began all over again. I heard Aunt Ada calling, but I couldn't answer. It was only when I felt I'd cried all the tears I had, that I was able to return to the house.

She took me by the hand. "Yolande, I'm so sorry. I said too much. Come on. I've got something that will make you feel better. Would you like that?" I nodded as she took my hand and led me to the piano, gesturing for me to sit next to her on the bench.

She smiled. "Now you turn the pages while I sing," she said.

As Aunt Ada sang—many of the songs the same ones I sang with Mama—I turned the thick, creamy pages. As always, the music wrapped its soft quilt of sound around my fears.

Later that night, when Mama called, I asked her about the things Aunt Ada had said.

"Your father and I love you so very much," Mama said. "Don't forget to say your prayers. God will make everything all right."

That wasn't the answer I wanted. I felt Mama was holding something back. But I knew better than to push. When Mama didn't want to talk about something, there was nothing to be done about it. So I decided to put my worries aside. And truthfully, it wasn't that hard. The long, light-filled afternoons were filled with Double Dutch with the neighborhood girls. And every evening we had lemonade and homemade peach ice cream and on Sunday, we sang in Aunt Ada's church.

Time passed quickly and before long it was July and Mama and Uncle Sax were pulling up in front of the house. When Mama gathered me up in her arms and her vanilla fragrance sweetened the air, I felt I'd died and gone to heaven.

The next morning, we piled into Uncle Sax's Buick. As we drove away, Aunt Ada and I blew kisses back and forth. I felt sad leaving her, but I was also eager to get back to St. Louis. I missed the museums and green parks, and the zoo. Most of all, I missed going with Daddy to hear the jazz musicians plucking their basses, guitars, and banjos and blowing their golden horns on the street corners.

In the mood to celebrate, I asked Mama to turn on the radio. When the sound of the big bands blared out, I yelled: "Right there! Leave it right there!" And for the next couple of hours, I swayed to the music as Kentucky's green and bluegrass fields rolled past the window.

When we crossed Interstate 55, the highway also known as the Double Nickel, my excitement rose. In my mind, I saw Daddy standing out front, waiting for us. But surprisingly, Uncle Sax turned onto a street I'd never seen before and parked the car in front of a squat, dingy two-story brick house. A peeling fence with missing slates surrounded a tiny, weed-choked yard.

I felt the familiar twist of worry. "Why are we stopping here? This isn't our house!"

Mama proudly announced, "It is now! Welcome to our new home!"

I couldn't believe what Mama was saying. Trash littered the street and the screen door dangled from its hinges. Dirt poked through the broken concrete steps leading up to the house. Mama explained the house was owned by Mr. and Mrs. Grady. They lived on the first floor; we would live on the second floor. Still, as much as I hated this house, another part of me didn't care about its ugliness. At least, we'd all be together again.

I burst through the screen door and charged up the stairs, eager to find Daddy.

All I found were two empty rooms.

In her soft voice Mama explained that though Daddy would no longer be living with us, he would visit a lot. I tried to wrap my mind around this terrible idea. Daddy—not living with us? How could that be?

"Mama, that can't be true! Daddy would never leave us!"

I wanted to keep the conversation going, but when I saw the tears in Mama's eyes, I fell silent.

And for awhile Daddy did visit—at least three times a month. Whenever he walked through the arched doorway, he knelt down and wrapped his lanky arms around us. And he always came with gifts—pajamas, white blouses and shirts, and squeaky, new school shoes. Even better, he read to us. I loved the sound of his booming voice, reciting the poems of

Langston Hughes. I especially loved the poem about the crystal stairs. And I thrilled to his voice going all gruff and growly when he read the part of the wolf in *Little Red Riding Hood*.

Still, as much as I loved Daddy's reading, I hated it too. Sometimes I couldn't enjoy his stories because I kept anticipating the end. The end of the story meant the end of Daddy's visit. No matter how much I begged him to stay he'd always explain that because he worked faraway he had to leave.

I was only eight at the time, but I knew that wasn't why he no longer lived with us. There was something about Daddy Mama just couldn't accept. I couldn't figure it out because Mama usually seemed happy during Daddy's visits. Sometimes she'd even cuddle up with him on the couch as we watched television.

But as time passed Mama seemed less and less happy during Daddy's visits. She stopped watching television with us and though she always let Daddy kiss us goodbye, she stopped kissing him before he left.

One night I woke up to the sound of yelling voices. I slipped out of bed and crouched near the living room door, slightly ajar. After a few minutes, Greg joined me.

Mama was standing in the middle of the room, her arms folded across her chest. "Jesse, I'm asking you to go back to the government job. I know what they did was not fair, but life isn't fair. You think I like sprinkling Tide and lotion into the bath water so the kids won't be afraid of getting into a rusted tub?"

Daddy snapped back. "You think I want my kids in a rusted tub? But what am I suppose to do? I'm not going to be someone's boy. Why can't you understand that? I want to leave here and go to England or Canada. I want you and the kids to come with me. We can start a new life while I write!"

Mama's voice rang out. "England, Canada? You can't make a living here. How are you going to support us as a *writer* in England?"

"That's exactly what I'm talking about. You won't even consider my dreams. As my wife, I'd like a little understanding and support!"

"Support? Support what?" Mama said. "The life of a writer with no guaranteed income? A life of you scribbling words on paper and hoping and waiting for your book to be published, while we move from ghetto to ghetto in a foreign country? I can't take this anymore, Jesse. We need stability."

Daddy sounded so angry I thought he'd explode. *"You* can't take it anymore? What about all the stuff I've had to put up with? But do I complain? No! I just put my head down and struggle to get ahead. I even fought for this country, putting my life on the line. And when I came back what did I get in return? Nothing but a porter's job on trains! I'm no better than a servant. I deserve more. And I intend to get it!"

Mama clenched her fists and said, "You deserve more? What about me? What about your children? I accepted it when you used our house savings to open the appliance store. And when the mob burned your store down, I stuck by you—even though we ended up in a flat with rats, roaches, and no heat! But I can't take it anymore, Jesse! I just can't.

11

It's over unless you change and go back to that job. You need to show me you care about me and the children."

"You know I care about you and the kids. That's why I opened the appliance store!"

Mama sat down on the arm of the couch, her face grim. "No," she said. "You did it for yourself. And you lost it all by yourself! So don't try to blame me for your bad decisions. If you weren't so busy wining and dining half the neighborhood, we wouldn't be in this mess."

Daddy laughed, a familiar, bitter laugh. A wave of nausea swept over me as he picked up a bottle of Jack Daniels, splashed it into a tumbler, and tossed it down. Mama remained sitting on the arm of the couch. And though her arms were locked across her chest, her mood suddenly shifted. "I think you've had enough to drink," she said quietly.

"And I think you're selfish and vindictive!" Daddy yelled back. "To get back at me, you steal my kids from me in the middle of the night and sneak away to Kentucky with my best friend Sax. Is that your idea of forgiveness?"

Mama slapped Daddy across the face and shoved him away from her, calling him a bastard. I was completely shocked. Mama never cussed or said such mean and ugly words. All my bones seemed to melt as I watched Daddy stumble backwards, crashing into a small table. My hands flew up over my ears. It felt like I was watching a monster movie.

Mama started to cry.

"Why can't you understand I love you and only you?" she said. "But after the fire, you became so bitter I couldn't talk to you anymore. And then the drinking started. And the staying out late. The writing at your desk all day long. I felt so alone. Not only did Sax listen to me, but he tried to help me understand your anger."

"How can you tell me you loved me, when you took my children away from me in the middle of the night?"

"What choice did I have? I couldn't talk to you!"

Unable to bear their quarrelling any longer, I stepped into the living room. "Mama what's wrong? Why are you and Daddy fighting?"

Escorting me back to bed, Mama quietly said, "We're not fighting, Baby. We're just talking.

Daddy trailed behind and when Mama began tucking me in, he tried to help.

But Mama wasn't having any of it. "Jesse! I want you to leave."

"No Daddy, don't go," I pleaded.

Daddy smiled. "I'm not going, Baby. I'll stay here with you until you go back to— "

Mama interrupted, her voice steely cold. "No, Jesse. You're not staying here. Get out. Now!"

Daddy snapped back, "These are my children, too. I'm not leaving."

Suddenly, a loud pounding sounded at the door. "Open up! Police!"

Daddy rushed back into the tiny living room and started pacing. Mama put her fingers to her lips and told us to stay in bed.

The pounding continued.

"Just a minute, I'm on my way," Mama called out. I trailed out after her.

"What's going on here?" one of the white men demanded as he stepped into the living room.

"Nothing officers," Mama said in low tones.

"We received a complaint from the landlord downstairs about a fight up here."

Mama shook her head. "No officers, we weren't fighting."

"I'd say some sort of disturbance went on here," the biggest policeman said, pointing to the overturned table.

The other heavy set policeman approached Daddy.

"What's your name Buddy?"

"Jesse Nicholson."

"What are you doing here, Jesse?"

Daddy stumbled over to the couch.

"Have you been drinking tonight Jesse?"

"Yes, I've had a couple of drinks. What's wrong with that? A man can't have a drink in his home?"

"Well Jesse, we're not clear this is your home. The landlord told us he rents these rooms to a woman and her children. Do you also live here?"

"No, but that's only because my wife and I are *temporarily* separated."

The policeman continued talking to Mama as if Daddy was invisible. "Is your husband responsible for this broken furniture? Mama looked at Daddy.

"Hey, don't look at him when I am talking to you!" the policeman said. "Did he hurt you?"

Before Mama could answer, Daddy sneered, "Did I hurt her? What are you trying to say? I came here to see my kids. So don't try to manufacture that I'm beating my wife!"

The biggest policeman moved towards Daddy, holding his Billy club, eyeing him with a look of pure hate.

"Watch your mouth. We're not asking you the questions. So shut up boy before we haul your black ass out of here!"

Daddy leapt up from the couch. "I'm not a boy! I'm a grown man, a husband, and a father!"

"Jesse, please, calm down. Don't do this," Mama said.

"Don't do what?" Daddy shouted, whirling around the room like a furious tornado. "Don't demand the respect I deserve? I'm not standing here, my head bowed, saying, 'Yes sah boss, you right Massa'! I fought for this country's freedom as an American! I'm not a black ass boy!"

Daddy hammered his fists against the wall. "I'm tired of taking this crap! I just want some respect. Like any other man!"

The big policemen rushed towards Daddy, grabbing his arms.

"Officers please let him go," Mama yelled. "He's just upset!"

The policeman tripped Daddy, causing him to topple forward. His head slammed against the floor. Next they pinned him down. Daddy started wildly kicking. The big policeman grabbed his arms, while the other snapped handcuffs around his wrists.

"Take these handcuffs off me! I haven't committed any crime!"

I called out for Mama. With blood streaming from his temples, Daddy raised his head.

"Julia, don't let them do this to me in front of my children! Call my lawyer!"

"Mama, don't leave us!" I shouted as she headed towards the door to go downstairs to the Grady's phone.

Daddy faced the policemen, thin ribbons of blood running down his cheeks. Suddenly, Daddy's whole mood changed. "Officers, I only came here to visit my family," he pleaded. "I brought my children clothes and shoes for their new school. I gave my wife money for groceries and rent. Why are you treating me like a criminal?"

The policemen didn't answer. Instead, they hauled Daddy to his feet and marched him out of the apartment. Mama swept past them and I followed behind.

The policeman escorted Daddy past the little knot of people that had gathered on the landing. "Come on man! Take these handcuffs off me," Daddy begged. "I swear I'll leave right now without any more turmoil."

"Officers, please!" Mama cried, breaking into tears. "I promise you there won't be any more trouble here!"

The shorter policeman answered. "Sorry lady, but it's not up to us. Your landlord called us with a complaint of peace disturbance on his premises. And frankly, your husband's had too much to drink. He's volatile. He resisted arrest. He's a threat to you and the people in this building."

Rushing up to Mr. Grady, who was standing with the others on the landing, Mama wept, "I'm so sorry for all of this confusion. He's just upset. It won't happen again."

"Yeah, I know it ain't gonna happen again, cause he and his sorry ass is goin' to jail for causing all this commotion," retorted Mr. Grady as he wiped the sweat from his coal-black face. "Not to mention you givin' me a bad reputation. I didn't rent you rooms expectin' this mess to happen."

"Mr. Grady, this won't ever happen again. Please, don't press charges."

He threw a chilling stare at Mama. "Well, let's put it this way. If I don't press charges, you and your kids have to go."

"Mr. Grady, my husband just paid you three months rent and we don't have anywhere else to go!"

"That ain't my problem. It's yours. Like I said, either he goes or you all go!"

Mama grabbed the rickety banister and collapsed. She called out in a low voice, "Jesse, I'm so sorry. God knows I didn't mean for this to happen."

She clasped her hands together. "Precious God, we need your help! What can I do, Lord?" Her plea evaporated into the humid air.

I sat beside Mama, clinging to her, trying to understand what happened. I shouted out to Daddy, "I love you. Please don't leave!"

Daddy paused at the foot of the steps and looked up at me with his sad, red eyes. "I love you too, Baby. Always remember that. Greg, help your mother with the kids."

"Okay, Daddy, I will," Greg answered, trying to sound manly.

The last thing I remembered was the sound of a wailing siren—loud at first, then growing softer as the car sped away into the night.

I put my head on Mama's knees. As she rocked me back and forth, she called out to God, her sobs turning into wails.

I wept too, calling out for Daddy.

***

After his release from jail, Daddy returned to his child-hood home in Memphis to work as a day laborer. I couldn't figure out why he did that. Daddy hated that job—probably as much as I hated school. Once I'd been a good student, but when Daddy left, I found myself daydreaming in class. My favorite daydream was the one in which Daddy met me after school. He would then beg pardon for leaving us. After forgiving him, I would climb into his shiny, black car with

Mama, my sister and brothers, and together we'd drive away from our ugly neighborhood.

But while the daydream had a happy ending, it came at the price of my schoolwork. When I read aloud, the kids snickered at me, whispering that I was stupid. On the playground, bullies teased me about being poor and some of the girls snatched me by the hair and pushed me against the walls. I felt like a cursed child who didn't belong anywhere. Not in my school and not at home even though Mama did everything possible to make our two miserable rooms cheerful.

She hung fresh white curtains on the smoky, streaked windows and scrubbed the floors to a dull shine. But everything was so old and worn it hardly made a difference. Embarrassed by the two dingy rooms, I never brought friends home. Even worse than the ugly rooms, was how I felt about Daddy. While I fiercely missed him, I hated him for leaving us behind in this ugly apartment. And I hated him for making me wait for his phone calls, which happened less and less over the years.

I felt the same way about the God Mama kept praying to.

I wanted to love him, but inside, especially as the years without Daddy dragged on, I couldn't understand why this huge, powerful man in the sky had sentenced my family to such a miserable life. Why did we deserve punishment like this? Why was Daddy gone, and why did my Mama have to work two jobs? During the day she was a secretary and in the evening, she cleaned up office buildings. Every night, she'd come home, completely exhausted.

But despite her fatigue, Mama never stopped trying to make the best of things. No matter that she worked day and night, she got up early every morning to press our clothes and make us hot buttered biscuits and steamy bowls of grits or oatmeal. After breakfast, she'd check our homework one final time then walk us to school. During those walks, she reminded us that every day is a gift. And that we should pray, sing, and work even in the face of troubles.

Hard though I tried to believe what Mama said, and do what she did, something inside me rebelled. I just wasn't like Mama who would never give up, especially when it came to her children.

One day when Mama and I were picking up our rugs at Washington Carpet Cleaners, the owner said to Mama, "Sure wish I had someone to help me clean up at the end of the day."

Mama jumped right in. "If you need help with cleaning, my oldest son, Greg is available. He's a good boy and a hard worker." Mama was a good sales person. By the time we left with our rugs, Greg had a job.

To reward Greg's hard work, Mama enrolled him in the Boy Scouts, determined to keep him off our dangerous streets.

With Greg and Mama both working, I was put in charge of picking up Jessica and Kevin from school. When I got home, I always stopped by Mrs. Grady's and called Mama on the phone, letting her know we'd arrived home safely. Although I didn't like Mr. Grady for sending Daddy to jail, I did like Mrs. Grady. Ever since that devastating night, she tried to make it up to Mama. Sometimes, after her family finished their Sunday meal, she'd come upstairs and offer Mama leftover fried chicken, with a big bowl of greens, and five slices of buttered pound cake.

One day, when I arrived home from school, Mrs. Grady handed me the phone.

As usual, Mama asked if I turned in all my homework. And as usual, I answered yes, though that wasn't really true. But then the conversation took a different turn. Mama told me to leave the kids with Mrs. Grady and go to the corner market to pick up a few items she'd pre-ordered at the grocery store.

I couldn't believe my luck!

I hung up the phone, raced upstairs, and changed out of my uniform. I loved walking outside without any responsibility for my brother and sister. This was when I could let my mind go wild. It was the time I imagined living in a big, beautiful house with summer barbeques in the backyard and an ebony piano in the living room, just like at Aunt Ada's.

The first part of my trip went smoothly and before long, I was on my way home, holding Mama's big sack of groceries. But as I neared the house, my stomach sank.

Billy June was playing craps on the curb.

At the sight of him, I recalled the day at the skating rink last month. Billy and his goon surprised me and my best friend, Veronica. While his goon taunted Veronica, Billy yanked me close and began licking my cheeks. I yelled for him to stop. In response, Billy shoved me against a wall and pushed me onto the ground. Somehow I managed to thrust my skates straight into his privates. Billy howled, and grabbing me around my neck, he began to squeeze. Luckily, an attendant pulled him off, threatening to beat him to a pulp if he ever returned to the rink. Billy slunk off, muttering that one day I would pay.

Well it seems that day had come—and much faster than I'd hoped. I picked up my pace, hoping Billy wouldn't see me.

It was too late.

"Hey Billy, look over there," his friend yelled. "It's her! That girl from the rink!"

Billy dashed across the street. "Hey you high yellow heifer, where you think you goin'?"

Clutching the grocery bags closer, I ran down the street as fast as my legs would take me.

"You think you gonna get away from me?" Billy yelled. "No, Bitch, today you die!"

He caught up with me easily. And darting ahead, he stuck out his leg, causing me to topple forward. As I did, the eggs, Spam, Wonder Bread, flour, powdered milk, beans, oatmeal, oranges, and bacon flew through the air and sprawled across the sidewalk. My face slammed straight into the crushed eggs.

From across the street, I heard a woman yell, "Stop it! Leave her alone!"

"Mind your own business!" Billy called back.

The woman shouted, "I'm calling the police."

Bullies like Billy had no fear of the police. Ignoring the threat, he yanked my head up and slapped me. His hand was like fire on my cheek.

"Look at you! Who's gonna help you now?" he sneered.

Scarcely able to breathe, I thought, "He's right, who's going to help me?" Mama and Greg are at work. Daddy's gone. Jessica and Kevin are too little. And I'd given up on God long ago.

Billy then swung his leg backwards, preparing to strike. I threw my arms over my head and crouched down, preparing for the worst. To my surprise he suddenly withdrew. Seeing my fear, he bent down over me. He pushed his face inches from mine. Holding my breath, I squeezed my eyes shut. Then, just like at the skating rink, I felt his tongue slither across my cheek. The stench of his foul breath and nasty saliva dripping on my skin was nauseating. As he backed off of me, proclaiming victory, I felt ready to vomit.

"That's your lesson for the day," he said. "It'll teach you to never mess with me again."

I realized I wasn't going to die. Not now. Not on this day.

But when Billy started laughing and kicking Mama's groceries into the street, my relief turned into raw rage. I bolted after Billy and jumping on his back, I dragged my fingernails across his pimply face.

Howling, he threw me off.

I charged into him again, this time tackling him so hard we both fell to the ground. I wrapped my arms around his neck, determined to choke the life out of him. He coughed and gasped for air as he struggled to pry my arms apart. I bit him on his ear making him squeal like a pig.

His friend drew near. "Billy...man...your face. It's bleeding!"

I slid quickly off his back, scrambled to my feet, and ran.

I heard Billy shout, "Shut up! Go catch her! Bring her back!"

Like a dog eager to obey his master, his friend sprinted after me. Though my legs were trembling, I just kept running and running until all of a sudden I heard a horn blare and the acrid smell of burning rubber filled my nose.

Next thing I knew, I was spinning through the air, a screen of stars blinking before my eyes, and after that, as if I were a character in some fast-forward movie, I found myself looking into Mrs. Grady's face. She was holding my head, dabbing at my cheeks with her apron.

"Be still," she whispered. "You're going to be all right." Those words seemed very far from reality; my head felt like it was going to burst apart. I heard someone say, "Did you get the license plate?"

I tried to hang on to the words swirling around me, but it was like trying to hold on to clouds. Something was wrapping itself around me, muffling me, taking me away.

Much later, I awoke to the sting of stitches and a familiar man's voice. It was Dr. Williams, our neighborhood family physician. "She's pretty lucky, Mrs. Nicholson. The gashes in her head will heal. She's going to be bruised for a little while but she's going to be just fine."

Mama leaned over me. "Yoli, you weren't just lucky today, you were blessed. It was the grace of God that saved you."

I couldn't speak, but weakly gestured for Mama to come closer. She placed her ear next to my swollen lips. "Mama," I whispered. "Can God save me from Billy again?"

Tears brimmed in Mama's eyes. "I don't want you to worry about that right now," she said, taking up my hand. "God protected you today. If you believe in him, The Almighty Lord will always be there for you."

She began reciting Psalms 23. "The Lord is my shepherd, I shall not want. He maketh me to lie down in green pastures..."

I wanted to believe Mama. I wanted to believe all this business about God being like a shepherd looking after his sheep. But I couldn't.

If God could stop Billy, why didn't He stop him today?

When Mama finished the psalm, she kissed me on my forehead.

"Baby, I'm so sorry you had to go through this. And because of this, I'm quitting my second job. From now on, I'll be home when school gets out."

I whispered back, "I'm sorry too. I tried my best to get home, but when he attacked me and kicked your groceries— I lost my temper! I needed to—"

Mama shushed me. "The only thing that matters to me is that you're alive. I thank God you are still here with me!"

I relaxed under her touch, feeling safe.

Who needed God? I had Mama.

Juliette Williamson
(Mama)

Jesse James Nicholson
(Daddy)

Juliette Williamson Nicholson & Jesse James Nicholson

Greg holding Jessica & Daddy holding Kevin

Yolande - Visitation HolyGhost School 1962

Greg, Yolande, Jessica, & Kevin Nicholson.

Kevin Nicholson – Visitation
Holy Ghost School

Jessica Nicholson
High School Photo

Rebecca & Aunt Ada

***

To take my mind off of Billy, Mama threw a party in my honor. She served up a swirly chocolate cake dotted with pink roses. Red streamers were taped across the archway of the door and bouquets of balloons bobbed around the kitchen table. After we'd eaten, Mama handed me a long, package wrapped in brown grocery paper tied up with a gold ribbon. I eagerly tore off the paper and when I caught sight of the gift inside, I gasped. Mama had bought me a violin! I snapped open the shiny clasps, and instantly, a fragrance like nutmegs and cloves scented the air. I rubbed my fingers across its glossy, tangerine colored wood. I'd never seen anything so beautiful.

Mama smiled. "You know I really want you to learn the piano—like Aunt Ada. But where on earth would we ever put a piano? Anyway, the violin's a beautiful instrument too. I know it's not new. I got it from Mr. Jack over at the pawnshop. But he polished it up a bit. The violin will be a fresh start. One day you'll play as good as Grandfather Dennis."

"Oh no, Mama!" I squealed. "I don't think so! I could never play like Grandpa Dennis!"

Mama smiled and told me not to worry. It seemed she'd made a special arrangement with Mr. Johnson from the Newstead Baptist Church to give me violin lessons. I knew all about Mr. Johnson from my friend Veronica. He'd once been a very talented piano man, but when his fingers curled up with arthritis, he began a tiny orchestra. He also taught some evenings at Newstead. But because Mama didn't want me walking to the church in the dark, she'd gotten Mr. Johnson to agree to come to our house.

"He's a generous man," Mama said, downplaying her own powers of persuasion. "He's offered to come to our house for only one dollar per lesson. Mama smiled more broadly. "I'm going to take in some ironing jobs so we can have him come at least two times a week."

I couldn't believe my luck. My own private music teacher!

So twice a week Mr. Johnson would climb our stairs and knock on our locked wooden door. With violin and bow in hand, I followed his bow legged body past our dreadful bathroom and down the narrow hallway to the makeshift cooking room for my lessons. And for once, the odd, ugly shape of our apartment worked in my favor. Because of the room's location, we had it all to ourselves.

Over the next few weeks, this little room with the humming icebox and rickety table and chairs, became my fairytale space. Or at least that's how I thought about it. I'd prop my music against a tall metal boiling pot, placing a couple of Royal Crown soda bottles on each side to keep it standing. Because Mama knew how important practicing was, she'd always hold off cooking until I was done.

"Filling up the spirit is just as important as filling up the belly!" she told me. Much as I loved my violin, I'm not sure I agreed, but I was glad Mama felt that way because it gave me time alone with my new instrument.

Under Mr. Johnson's soft-spoken instruction, I was soon able to coax out a sound. Bowing away on those four delicate strings, even before I knew how to finger, led me into a private dreamland—a place far from the noise and chaos outside our windows. Sunk in music-making, I forgot about the trashy lots. I forgot about the boarded up, burned out buildings. With each scale, I erased the sickening site of girls not much older than me being led away by sleazy pimps.

Still the violin couldn't take me far enough away from thoughts about Billy.

"Don't worry," Greg told me one night after supper when Mama announced I'd have to return to school. "I'm going to make everything all right. Billy the Beast won't be bothering you anymore."

I didn't really know what he meant by that but the next day, when he didn't come home from his job at the cleaners, I suspected it had something to do with Billy.

I said nothing, even though Mama sat near the window, anxiously peering through the lace curtains, praying to God to bring Greg safely home.

When Greg finally arrived, Mama was waiting for him at the top of the stairs, hands squarely on her hips.

"Where've you been? Washington Carpet told me you left a long time ago."

"Delayed, Mama. That's all."

Mama narrowed her eyes. "Delayed? Delayed where? And you better not lie to me!"

Greg looked down. "I was with my friends at Shorty's pool hall. I didn't know it was this late. I'm sorry, I didn't mean for you to worry."

"You didn't mean for me to worry? What did you think I was going to do when you didn't arrive home on time? And you know I've forbidden you to hang around the pool hall. When I tell you to come home after work I expect you to obey! Do you understand?"

Greg raised his eyes. "Yes Ma'am, I understand."

Mama was still in a fiery mood, but she told Greg to go and wash for dinner.

Later that evening, I came back upstairs to get a glass of Kool-Aid. I couldn't resist asking Greg what happened.

He looked at me for a long moment and then said, "You don't have to worry about Billy anymore. He got his butt kicked today."

I felt a strange mix of relief and disbelief. "Ooooh Greg, you lied to Mama and got into a fight with Billy! If she finds out you are going to be in big trouble!"

"I didn't lie to her and I didn't get into a fight with Billy. But Ronnie and Melvin did me a favor. They roughed him up a little. But this has got to be our secret. He then returned to his book, signaling the end of the conversation.

I had to stop and think. I didn't much like Greg lying to Mama, but in the end I promised Greg I wouldn't breathe a word. I knew Mama would be really mad, especially because one of her favorite things was to remind us that getting even wasn't our privilege. On more than one occasion, Mama quoted her Bible—"Vengeance is mine, sayeth the Lord!" But honestly, since Mama's God wasn't protecting me from Billy, I was grateful to Greg for doing the job.

I raced back outside and joined in a neighborhood game of Double Dutch. And as I skipped in the flurry of the ropes clapping against the cobble stones, I rejoiced in the thought of Billy getting what he deserved.

Later that evening, I poured all my happiness into my playing. Even when Mama ordered me to bed, I kept right on making music. I created a song in my head with pounding piano chords and fast fiddling sounds that made Billy spin around and around, faster and faster, until he evaporated into nothingness.

And I think that music followed me straight into my dreams because the next morning when I awoke, I still felt happier than I'd been in a long, long time.

***

But though I no longer feared Billy, I soon had a new worry. Mama's beautiful, sculpted legs were changing right before my eyes. Each week, they grew weaker and thinner, and by the time I turned twelve, they had become so frail she had to use a cane just to get around the house.

Despite her handicap, Mama's care for us never wavered. I loved charging down the stairs after school to meet her on the landing below, her braced leg propped against the railing. And I loved hearing the other kids say: 'Your mother's so pretty' and then teasingly add, 'So what happened to you?'

But when they asked about her legs, I exploded in anger. "That's for me to know and for you to never find out!" Not that I knew. I had no idea why Mama's leg was caged up in a metal bar with an ugly, brown, lace-up shoe stuck on the end.

But Mama never complained.

I don't know what made her so strong. She'd grown up in Denmark County of Jackson, Tennessee and worked on the family farm. She was the sixteenth child from a family of eighteen. Her father, Dennis Williamson, was born a slave and was freed by his father, the slave master, when he was seven years old. Mama told us that Papa Dennis had worked all of his young life in the big house and in the fields. But when he became an adult, he was among the very few freed slaves who owned over 100 acres of land in Tennessee. He was a carpenter, brick mason, tailor, and business owner. He also built the first small Negro church and school house in their rural community. Mama and her brothers and sisters went to church to sing, play the piano, and to read and recite scripture several times a week. When Mama told me these stories, I began to understand her special relationship to God and music. Both were part of her family. And though Mama enrolled us in a Catholic school, she also made us go to Newstead Baptist Church in the afternoon. This was her way of making sure that we didn't lose the connection to the God of her father's church.

Still Mama wasn't all serious. She believed in fun too. That's why, at the end of each week, she took us to the Visitation-Holy Ghost church's Friday night fish fry. After supper, we joined the others for a night of skating in the church's basement roller rink.

I loved thundering around the wooden floor as Motown and Doo Wop, Smokey Robinson and the Miracles and Frankie Lyman blared through the speakers. Whenever I took a tumble, Mama—who always sat on the side of the rink with Kevin and Jessica—would throw up her hands in mock horror. As soon as I scrambled back up on my feet, she'd wildly laugh and clap.

One Friday night, after returning from the rink, Mama called us all into her room. She then asked Greg to pull two big boxes out of the closet and put them on the bed.

"Well, don't just stand there," she said, broadly smiling. "Open them!"

We tore through the paper, lifted the flaps, and lifted out new bedspreads and crisp white sheets.

"For your bedrooms," Mama proudly announced. "When school ends, we're moving to a new home."

My heart quickened. Not only were we getting all these pretty linens, but we were moving from the two rooms I hated!

When moving day finally arrived, and Uncle Henry, Frank, and Lonnie drove us through our new neighborhood, my eyes widened in wonder. No trash littered the streets. There were no vacant or boarded up buildings. No heaps of broken beer bottles. And when the truck and car stopped in front of a two family brick house with a manicured lawn, I felt I'd died and gone to heaven. Between her ironing and at-home bookkeeping jobs, Mama had managed to save up enough money to get us into this pretty neighborhood.

I rushed inside, discovering an apartment with six spacious rooms, plenty of closet space, a kitchen, and private bath. Out back was a big, fenced in yard. For the longest time I stood in that yard, listening to the birds calling. And as I gazed up at the aqua sky, dotted with high, puffy white clouds, something inside me changed.

For the first time, I found myself believing in Mama's God.

Maybe everything was really going to be all right now.

But in less than three weeks, my belief in Mama's God vanished completely. I was happily spooning oatmeal into my mouth when the faith-shattering words arrived.

"Yolande, The Helpers of the Holy Souls convent has a summer program for young girls. I've signed you up to attend. Uncle Frank will be taking you there next week. It's an excellent summer school opportunity. If you successfully complete the program, you'll be able to return every summer until you graduate from high school."

I stared at Mama in disbelief. "I don't want to go to the convent! Girls who go there have to become nuns! "

"I already spoke with Father Peete. We think this will be a great experience for you. And besides you'll be with girls your age and make new friends from other neighborhoods."

"I don't want to make new friends!"

"You say that every time we move," Mama laughed. "But then you met Jackie and now the two of you are best friends."

"But I'm going by myself. None of my friends will be there."

"Well the nice thing about this summer program is sometimes you can have visitors on the weekend. It won't be as bad as you think."

"I don't care! I don't want to go!" I retorted emphatically. "I want to stay home! I don't want to be a nun! And if you make me go, I'll run away."

Mama's face remained soft. "Yolande, you're being hard headed and stubborn. You need to be in a safe place where you can learn and grow." Mama's tone then shifted, becoming playful. "And don't think I haven't noticed Jonathan is stopping by the house more than ever. I think he likes you."

I couldn't believe Mama was saying such things. She sounded like Jackie, my best friend, who three weeks earlier, reported that Jonathan was planning to take me skating. But now that would never happen because I was being shipped to a convent.

"Why are you doing this to me? Why are you sending me away?"

Mama looked at me a long while and then said, "I'm not sending you away. You'll be back before you know it. And the convent is only a few miles from home. In fact, it's down the street from the Sinclair gas station."

Sensing she was making little progress, Mama changed tactics. "At least at the convent, I can be certain you'll focus on your mind, not your behind."

I didn't find Mama's little rhyme the least bit amusing. And I told her so.

Mama's smile disappeared. "Now you listen to me young lady. You're stepping over your boundary. No more conversation. It's settled. You're going to the convent summer program. The sooner you accept this, the better."

Accept, accept, accept. It's all I was ever asked to do. Accept the convent. Accept that Daddy was gone. Accept that Mama's legs were getting weaker every single day. Accept that I belonged to a poor, powerless, and cursed race.

I was tired of accepting.

And in that moment, I vowed I would no longer accept, but triumph. And the world would be watching.

**

On orientation day, the Mother Superior, a small woman with gin-blue eyes, let us know exactly who was in charge.

"Attention, girls!" she commanded in a voice bigger than her small size. The chatter died down at once, though a handful of girls next to me kept right on talking. I turned around and placing my finger across my lips, I loudly shushed them.

Mother Superior pointed in my direction.

"What's your name?"

"Yolande," I mumbled.

"Speak up and say your name again!"

"Yolande."

"Spell it."

"Y-O-L-A-N-D-E."

"Oh, it's Yolanda," she said, deliberately mispronouncing my name. "Well, Yolanda, I don't need your assistance to achieve silence or order. So please refrain from shushing everyone. Do you understand?"

I nodded, thinking that this was going to be a very, very long summer.

"Good," she said. "Now let's continue."

She then began describing what we could expect at the convent. Every morning after Mass, we were to read the chart posted outside the cafeteria. From this chart, we'd learn our assignments. At the end of each week, a silver star would be placed next to the names of the girls who'd performed well. And if our work was really good, we'd get a gold star. And if we didn't receive a star, we'd have to repeat the task until we did.

Mother Superior mechanically smiled. "Have I made myself clear?" she said.

"Yes, Mother Superior," the girls replied in unison.

In that moment, I knew that the only way I was going to get through this summer was to avoid Mother Superior at all cost.

Still, bad as Mother Superior was, the convent turned out to be a little better than I had imagined.

In my first week, I was assigned yard work. I was grateful for this. It was wonderful to be in the warm air and not stuck inside the house. I did my task diligently and at week's end, received a silver star. As much as I thought I didn't care about Mother Superior's silly charts, that little star made me happy.

During my second week, an instructor came and taught us how to make simple meals like baked chicken, spaghetti and meatballs, deviled eggs, omelets, and pancakes. I did well at this too. In fact, everything was going along smoothly until catechism class at the end of the week.

As usual, Mother Superior was preaching to us about how much God loved us.

"God, our Father, loved us so much that he sent us his only begotten Son, Jesus. It is because of the blood of Jesus and his suffering for us that we have eternal life. And if you choose Jesus as your savior, your suffering will not be in vain. You will receive your just reward in heaven. God only wants the best for you."

Finding all this hard to swallow, I raised my hand. "Mother Superior, if God loves us all, why do some people have so much before they get to heaven and others have so little?"

"What do you mean?"

"It seems like God plays favorites. I don't believe He loves everybody the same."

Her pasty face flushed. "Of course He does! Why would you say a thing like that?"

"Because it doesn't seem fair that some people have plenty of food, clothes, and nice houses while others work so hard to just get by."

She looked like she'd been stung by a big, bad bee. "You can't blame that on God! First of all, God does not play favorites. And secondly, are you referring to your mother?"

I shifted uncomfortably in my seat. "Yes, but also my father and other people I know who work so hard."

"Well, I understand that your mother is unable to work and is receiving state aid," she said. "While I don't know about your father, I know it isn't God's fault that some men don't take care of their families. The Bible clearly states that a man's duty is to support his family."

As Mother Superior spoke, a part of me wanted to argue, to set her and everyone else in the room straight about Daddy. He wasn't some lazy man who didn't care about his family. He worked as a porter on the trains, bowing his head and shining the shoes of white men who saw him as less than a human being. Daddy had been a soldier too—putting his own life on the line so everyone could enjoy the freedom he was denied.

But another part of me had no wish to defend Daddy. Truth is he *had* left his family. With this recognition, my heart burned with the familiar mix of guilt and shame and anger.

The beginning of the third week was more of the same—chapel, chores, and boredom. On the third weekend, though Mama couldn't come and visit on account of her bad legs, we spoke on the phone.

"I want to come home," I pleaded. "I've been here long enough. I can't go anywhere or do anything. I might as well be in jail!"

Mama laughed. "That's' a bit of a stretch. You certainly aren't in jail."

"Well it feels like jail to me. I've done everything you and the nuns asked me to do. So I am hoping you could talk with Mother Superior and convince her you need me at home."

"Yoli, you have to stay for the entire summer to receive your certificate. Without that, you won't be eligible for next year."

I couldn't believe what I was hearing. "Next year! No way! I don't want to be eligible for next year."

Mama answered, "Yolande, let's just take one summer at a time. All you have to do is make it through the next few weeks. I know you can do this."

I hated it when Mama tried to shame me into doing the right thing. It reminded me of how she tried to convince Daddy to return to the government job he hated.

That's when I hit on a plan: If I had to endure the convent, than the convent would have to endure me.

My first opportunity came when I was put in charge of supper duty. I decided to create my own special recipe. Instead of only using mayonnaise, I squeezed a half a tube of Colgate toothpaste into the pale yellow yolks and whipped them up until they were nice and creamy. I filled the boiled egg whites with my special filling. I also mixed half a can of cayenne pepper into the meatballs.

Later I enjoyed the fruits of my labor. As a matter of fact, I enjoyed them so much that I had to bury my face in my pillow to hide my laughter as the girls scurried back and forth to the bathroom all night, emptying their bodies of the terrible supper I'd prepared.

The next morning, Mother Superior grilled me and the two other girls on the dinner shift. By then I was feeling a little remorseful, so I explained that I might have mistakenly added too much red pepper to the meatballs. Mother Superior stared at me for a long moment and then said, "Yolande, I'm putting you in charge of pressing the nun's habits."

This job made dinner detail seem like a snap. The work was steamy and tedious and made me want to leave the convent more than ever. Each night, I'd draw a big X on my wall calendar, counting down the days until I could return home. To spite Mother Superior, I even scorched a habit now and then, taking victory in leaving crisp, brown burn marks on the snow white cloth.

Still, despite my pranks, I felt duty bound to be serious in chapel.

Maybe it's because I could hear Mama's voice in my head. Somehow I knew that being disrespectful in chapel was an affront to her deeply spiritual self.

Along with Mass, we had to adhere to private meditations. The nuns explained that if we sincerely prayed, God would break the silence and make his voice heard. But God never spoke to me. I didn't expect anything different.

God was silent on the day Daddy was taken away. He said nothing when Mama's beautiful legs grew weaker, and he was awfully quiet on the day when Billy beat me up. Why would He bother to speak to me now?

But I was willing to give Him another chance.

Thinking I was doing something wrong, I began kneeling next to Margaret Mary. In my eyes, Margaret Mary was a snitch and a brown noser who floated around the convent wearing a self-appointed halo. But brown noser or not, she seemed to know how to pray because she announced that God had spoken to her at least three times. After watching her for several days, I chalked her success up to the fact that she fingered her rosary beads with incredible speed.

So I started going fast too—deliberately skipping glass beads. But it made no difference; no heavenly voice broke open in my ears.

One day, during silent time, I leaned over to Margaret Mary. "Is God speaking to you right now?"

Keeping her gaze straight ahead, she nodded.

I moved closer. "What's He saying?"

This time, she turned away from me.

"Come on, Margaret Mary," I insisted. "What's He saying?"

Again, she didn't answer.

But an answer was on its way. Just not the one I wanted.

I looked up and saw Mother Superior sweeping down the aisle. When she reached my pew, she looked down at me with narrowed eyes.

"Yolanda," she said, spitting out my name like it was poison. "Follow me. Out of the chapel. Now."

My heart pounding, I trailed behind her. When we entered her office, she motioned for me to sit. She then moved behind her desk chair and for the longest time, stared out of the big window overlooking the yard. Through the glass, I could see black clouds piling up in the sky.

I gazed around the room.

Pictures of sad-eyed saints hung on the wall and on her desk, a letter opener lay next to a container of sharpened pencils. Dusty notebooks were stacked on the windowsill. There was absolutely nothing soft or pretty about Mother Superior's office.

I braced myself for the worst.

After settling into her burgundy chair and adjusting her wireframe glasses, she leaned across the desk, her blue eyes digging into me like ice-picks.

The interrogation began.

"Young lady, I know you remember there is a rule of silence in the chapel. But it appears you've willfully decided to be disobedient. Do you think that's a good thing?" The heat in my face rose and behind my eyes, I saw an image of Daddy being handcuffed and led out of the apartment.

At once, I grasped its meaning.

Like Daddy, I, too, had had good intentions. And like Daddy, I knew I was going to be completely misunderstood.

Terrified, I said nothing.

Mother Superior took a deep breath and continued. "Your silence indicates that we have a serious problem here. So I'll repeat my question."

I tried to pay attention to what Mother Superior was saying, but the sound of thunder, now rumbling in the distance, distracted me. It seemed God was finally talking to me. I replied, "I heard what you asked, but I don't understand what you mean by a serious problem."

Beet colored spots splotched her starchy, wrinkled cheeks. A forked vein throbbed in her temple.

"You don't understand what I mean by a serious problem?" she echoed, mimicking my voice. "Don't sit there and play games with me! I asked you a direct question and I want a direct answer! Why were you talking during silent hours?"

I sat up straighter. "We've been told that if we pray daily, God will speak to us. And I've been praying really hard during chapel. But I've never heard the voice of God. Not at home. And not in this convent. Seems He's just not paying attention to me. Since Margaret Mary's a good prayer, I thought she could tell me how to get God to talk to me."

Mother Superior hit the desk hard with her clenched fist, making the pencil's rattle in their holder. "What do you take me for, a fool?" she said, her thin face turning deep red. "This convent is not a joke. We take the work of God seriously. We've given our lives to live in this poor neighborhood and teach colored people how to live in the grace of our Lord and Savior. And you have the audacity to sit here and lie to me about why you were talking during silence hours! If you're praying correctly God will speak to you. God's not the problem! You are. And don't think I haven't noticed that several undergarments have been burned. Not to mention the day you *accidently* over seasoned the meatballs!"

"But," I added quickly, "I was only—"

"No more buts young lady! You always have some flimsy excuse for your inappropriate behavior."

My mind shut down. All I could see was her mouth moving. I was sincere about what happened in chapel with Margaret Mary. I really wanted to communicate with God because I had a lot of questions. But it didn't matter.

She didn't believe me.

She never had.

She never would.

I blurted out: "Mother Superior, I was just trying—"

"I've heard enough! Because of this recent insolence and the other times you've joked around and audaciously questioned the way of God—you won't be permitted to join the others for dinner meals next week. You'll leave your room only for breakfast, chapel, and chores!"

Back in my room, I threw myself across the bed, hot, angry tears stinging my eyes. My pranks had backfired. Instead of freeing me from the convent, they'd driven me into solitary confinement.

Seeing little recourse, I changed tactics.

All the next week, I completed my assigned chores without incident. And during the long hours alone in my room, I played my violin. It had become my refuge—a beautiful island among the endless waves of fear, anger, and sadness that battered my heart.

When my week of isolation ended, Mother Superior allowed me to rejoin the others at dinner. I was surprised when she stopped by my place and made a nice comment about my violin playing. It seems she'd been listening outside of my door.

To my surprise, she sat next to me and in a wistful voice said, "You know, Yolanda, before I joined the convent I dreamt of being a pianist."

I nodded politely, but inside I felt complete indifference. I didn't want to hear about Mother Superior's stupid dreams. My dislike of her and the convent had turned into full blown hatred. I wanted one thing and one thing only—out.

And that's exactly what I told my friend Jackie when she came to visit.

"You know, Yoli, none of us believed you would have lasted this long," Jackie said as we sat cross legged in the court yard, catching up. "We actually put bets on you. We figured if you made it through the first two weeks you'd become a lifer."

I snorted. "That's so stupid! I'd never choose being in a convent as a life goal. I'm only here because Mama signed me up. After this summer, I'm done!"

Jackie shook her head. "Girl, don't you know that if you make it through half of the program, you'll never get out? You'll be guaranteed a spot for next summer. And the summer after that. I tell you—you're gonna be a lifer! You're gonna be a nun!"

Jumping to my feet, I shot Jackie a dirty look. "Never!" I insisted, surprised at the power in my voice. "And you can tell that to everyone else!"

"Sure, I'll tell them. But no one's going to believe me."

"They won't have to believe you. I'll tell them my-self!"

"How you gonna do that?"

"When we go skating."

"Yoli, the rink closes next Saturday. And you still have two more weeks to go in this place!"

My anger drained away, replaced by anxiety. "Are you sure?"

"Course I'm sure. We're all meeting on Friday for our end of summer skating party."

"Okay...fine...then I'll have to figure out a way to get to the rink before it closes for the summer."

"Are you crazy? There is no way you can do that."

I made a face. "Wanna bet? Next Friday, I want you to bring me a pair of slacks, a blouse, and a pair of socks. Meet up with me at the Sinclair gas station. I'll change my clothes in the bathroom. We'll then walk over to the rink and I'll set everyone straight."

Jackie protested loudly. "You're not dragging me into this! I'm not missing the last skating party. Besides, you can't get out of here without being seen!"

I grabbed Jackie's hands. "Please! I can't stand it here. I need to get out, even for just a few hours. Come on, Jackie! When you asked me to cover for you when you snuck out to meet Kenny at the movies, did anyone find out? No! I covered for you because you're my best friend and that's what friends are for. Promise me you're going to be at the station."

Triumph was mine. Reluctantly, she agreed.

All the next week, I cheerfully went about my chores. I didn't even grumble when I was given extra loads of laundry. And when Friday night finally arrived, I retreated to my room after dinner and prayers. Once the convent feel silent, I stuffed my pillows with the extra habits I'd been stockpiling all week from the laundry room.

After bunching the pillows under the blankets in the shape of a body, I stepped into the hall and quietly made my way to the basement. At the top of the stairs, I snapped on the switch and removed a battery-powered flashlight from a small toolbox attached to the wall. I inched down the stairs, headed to the outside door, and turned the knob.

It didn't open.

I leaned my whole body against it and pushed.

Still nothing.

My mind started to race. Had someone locked it from the other side? Did someone else know about my plan? Had Jackie betrayed me?

I swung my flashlight wildly through the basement's darkness. Catching sight of an unlatched window, I climbed onto the washing machine and wiggled my way through. Once outside, I darted across the convent lawn and when I reached the southwest corner of the building, I shimmied up over the chain link fence. Hitting the pavement, I ran like a star sprinter.

Free!

As planned, Jackie was standing in front of the Sinclair station, clutching a bag. I waved to her as I crossed the street. Her lower jaw dropped. "I can't believe you got out!"

"I told you my plan was fail proof!" I boasted, very pleased with myself for pulling this off. "So did you tell anybody I was coming?"

"No one," she said.

"Great. Now let me get ready. Can't wait to see the faces on everyone who betted I'd be a lifer. Thirteen and a half year old girls that run away in the night aren't lifer material!"

When we reached the rink, everyone was curious.

"What's your daily schedule?"

"How does it feel to be locked away?"

"Do you have to remain silent?"

"Is it true you only eat one meal a day?"

"What's it like to live with the nuns?"

After patiently answering their questions, I laced up my skates and happily began rolling around the rink to the sounds of Motown. I even got asked to skate on couples only. I imagined how great Jonathan and I looked as we glided around the rink together.

But as the evening wore on, I knew I was pushing my luck. I needed to get back to the convent or risk getting caught.

My friends accompanied me to the Sinclair station and, after changing I hoisted myself over the chain link fence and dashed across the convent lawn. As before, I squeezed through the basement window and headed upstairs to my room, all the while congratulating myself for pulling off this amazing feat.

But when I opened the door, my heart dropped and I could feel warm pee trickling down my leg. Mother Superior was sitting on the chair next to my bed, her face and habit reflecting the red traffic light flashing through the window.

"Where have you been!" she demanded, spitting out each word.

"I'm sorry," I whispered.

"What did you say?" she demanded.

"I'm *so* sorry."

"I am *so* sorry" she said, mimicking my tone. "Do you think those empty words absolve you from your disrespect for our rules?"

"Mother Superior, I'm *truly* sorry. I know I made a mistake. I didn't mean to be disrespectful. I just can't take it anymore. I needed to see my friends."

I waited for her to explode, but instead she flipped on the light switch and shaking her head, fastened her eyes on me.

"I don't know what to do with you," she said. "I've tried to help you fit into our way of living, but you refuse to follow the rules. You're a good worker, and you always take on additional chores to help others. But you have an untamed spirit that keeps getting in the way. You can't just follow

54

some of the rules *some* of the time. You can't pick and choose."

"But I can't become a nun like you!"

"I know that. But that still does not excuse your behavior tonight. Where did you go?"

"I went to the skating rink."

"What if something had happened to you tonight? You know how dangerous it is for a young girl to be out on the streets alone."

"I wasn't alone. I was with my friends. And I made it back."

"That's not the point. You decided your personal goals are more important than the convent's goals. While waiting in here for you, I contemplated your termination. But I've decided not to do that. You'll finish out your final week of the program. But I'll let your mother and Father Peete know that you'll not be recommended for next year."

I tried to remain serious because I knew this was a serious situation. But inside, I felt the flush of victory. God had finally heard me and answered my prayers. I was getting out and never coming back!

"Do you understand?"

"Yes, Mother Superior, you're right," I nodded, trying my best to sound contrite.

In spite of herself, she chuckled. "So you think I'm right? Well now that's a first. But I'm not letting you off the hook so easily. You still have one last duty before you leave.

I want you to play your violin at the closing ceremony this Friday night."

All feelings of victory vanished. This was almost as bad as being expelled. I dreaded the idea of standing in front of the others, my awkwardness on display.

"I'm not ready," I protested. "I'd be too embarrassed." She sat down next to me.

"My intent isn't to embarrass you. I want to show the others that your talent is best suited for a life outside of our walls. You can do this. I know it. You can tell me your decision tomorrow."

After she left, I cleaned up and sank into bed, my heart pounding. Whatever Mother Superior thought, she was wrong. I could not do this. I could not play in front of the whole convent. My worries followed me into sleep. I dreamt I was standing in the cafeteria, my arms frozen to my sides. No matter how hard I tried, I could not lift them. But then, right before I woke up, I had another dream.

In this dream, Daddy was sitting at his typewriter. He was wearing his soldier's uniform, pounding away on the ebony keys. In the next frame, Mr. Grady burst through the door, grabbed the typewriter, and threw it on the floor. Daddy yelled in disbelief. Two policemen rushed in and clamped handcuffs around Daddy's wrists. As they dragged him out the door he howled, "I'm a writer! I am not a criminal!"

Next, Mama appeared. She was waiting at the bottom of the stairs, her caged leg propped up on the railing. She unclamped the bars around her legs, stood up and stretched out her arms. Her eyes were full of light. "Come on, Yoli," she called out. "Let's go outside and play!"

I heard myself protest: "Mama you can't do Double Dutch! You can barely stand!"

"What are you talking about?" she said. "I can stand perfectly fine on my own, just like you. I can jump rope all day long. Come on! What are you waiting for? Let's go!"

She ran out of the door. I stared in disbelief. How did she do that? The doctors said she would never walk freely again. But it seemed the doctors were wrong. In the distance I heard Mama singing and laughing as the ropes tapped against the cobblestone.

When I opened my eyes, I realized one thing: God might have chosen to remain silent, but Mama and Daddy had spoken to me loud and clear.

That morning, I told Mother Superior about my decision.

"Good! I'm so glad you decided to play in the recital," she beamed. "Anne Marie will play the piano, three other novices are going to sing two hymns, and you will play your violin."

"Uh…Mother Superior?"

"Yes."

"Did you call my mother or Father Peete to tell them that I won't be getting a certificate?"

"No. I decided to wait on that," she said. "There's only four days to complete the program. Unless you decide to run away, burn more habits or spice up our dinner, you'll be going home on Saturday, certificate in hand."

It was official. I would never have to come back to the convent!

I breezed through the final days finishing my daily chores, even getting a few silver stars by my name. Between chores and practicing, the week flew by and finally, the night of the concert arrived.

Mother Superior opened the evening with a prayer. Next, Anne Marie played the piano and the trio of novices sang hymns, concluding with Mother Superior's favorite, *Ave Maria.*

When my turn came, I twisted and tightened my pegs, tuning the strings. I then tucked the violin beneath my chin, curling my hand around its thin neck. Drawing my bow across the strings, I broke the uncomfortable silence.

At first, I felt self-conscious, held hostage by the audience. But as I warmed to the music, my awkwardness melted away. Before long, my mind and body were totally absorbed in the music I was making. I felt like I was dancing with sound.

When I'd finished, there was a long silence.

It seemed the only one who liked my playing was me.

But then to my surprise, a burst of applause exploded in my ears. Mother Superior and all my convent sisters stood up, one after another.

Even Margaret Mary smiled at me! And even more shocking, Mother Superior came to the stage and gave me a clumsy little hug.

At the end of the program, I called Mama on the telephone.

"Mama, I'm done! My recital went well and I got my certificate! I'm coming home in the morning!"

"Congratulations! I wish I could have been there," Mama said. "I know you didn't want to do any of this—but you did and very successfully. I love you and am so proud!"

"I love you too, Mama. But I'm not sure you're going to be so proud of me after I get home."

"Why wouldn't I be?"

"Mama, I don't want you to be upset or disappointed, but I'm not coming back next year."

There was a long pause before Mama spoke on the other end. "Why not?"

"Because Mother Superior and I agreed I'm not cut out for this life. Besides, I don't want to be a nun!"

"Honey, I know you don't want to be a nun! That was never my intention."

"Then why did you make me go through all of this?"

"I wanted you to have a new experience. An experience that could help you grow. And it sounds like you did just that."

While I wasn't quite sure I agreed with Mama, I hung up the phone feeling pretty good nonetheless. Who knows?

Maybe one day I'd not just be a cafeteria violinist, but a real one, playing on the stages of the world.

Like Mama always said, 'anything is possible!' And for the first time, I began to believe she just might be right.

***

When I returned to my neighborhood, my new found belief quickly faded. My friends mocked me: "Girl, you went to that convent and lost your mind! Do you really think you're gonna get out of here? So you played your violin in a cafeteria for a bunch of nuns. That don't make you special. You'll always be stuck here just like the rest of us." Their comments stung. What if they were right? What if all of the hours of drawing my horse-haired bow across four delicate strings came to nothing?

If that wasn't bad enough, the neighborhood was changing.

It was not unusual to see junkies in vacant lots, lounging on rotting sofas nodding off. Or fourteen year old girls stashed in the corners of alleyways, their bodies pressed up against black-suited well-to-do men twice their age.

Mama had grown weaker too, stuck much of the day in her wheel chair. But she refused to embrace the idea of hopelessness and defeat. She always reminded us, "It is not *what* you go through, but *how* you go through it."

Encouraged by my success with the violin, Mama enrolled me in the newly formed orchestra started by Sisters Jerome and Leon Marie. She even took in extra book keeping work and more ironing jobs, determined to pay for my sheet music and extra lessons.

Like Mama, Sister Jerome and Sister Leon Marie were very strong women. Sister Jerome was the first black nun I'd ever known. She was a trained musician who played the piano and violin like Mr. Johnson. Sister Leone Marie sang like an angel with an Irish accent.

One day at the end of our rehearsal for the winter concert, Sister Jerome approached me. "Yolande, you've improved so much that we've decided to promote you to first chair."

And there was more. Sister Jerome wanted me to audition for a scholarship to attend St. Marks, a private high school for girls. She was certain I could get a music scholarship.

"Sister Jerome, what do you mean by an audition?" I asked.

"An audition is when you compete with other students for the chance to enter this school. You're judged on your musical skill and talent."

My old terror returned. "Sister Jerome, I don't want to go to another high school. I have to attend Sumner High."

"What do you mean; you *have* to go to Sumner High?"

"I won't fit into the school you're talking about. I am just an average student. I'm not smart enough to go to that kind of school!"

She smiled warmly. "Yes you will. St. Marks is looking for talented students like you. You've got musical talent and your grades are sufficient."

"But what if I audition and they don't accept me! Everyone will know I failed!"

She handed me a couple of sheets of paper. "Just take this application home and discuss it with your mother. It's your decision."

Later that evening, Mama and I poured over the application. Mama came to a conclusion pretty quickly. She wanted me to try out for the school.

This was even worse than Mama's decision to send me to the convent.

"I don't want to disappoint you, but I don't want to apply or audition for this school," I protested. "It's mostly white kids. I just want to go to Sumner High. Like the rest of my friends."

Mama sighed. "Sumner High School has a good band program, not an orchestra. If you want to continue to play your violin, you'll still have to apply for another school. Besides, this school is offering a scholarship program, which would help cover the cost of your tuition."

"I'm scared. I don't think I can do this! You think I can, but I don't think I can! These people don't know me like you and Sisters Jerome and Leon Marie."

Without answering, Mama pushed away from the table. She rolled past me, squeezing her wheelchair through the narrow bedroom door. I trailed behind. She then parked her wheelchair near her dresser and withdrew a small metal box. Putting it on her lap, she sifted through the pictures.

She held up a small, grainy photo. Her dark hair framed her face and her blue dress matched the sky.

"This is one of my favorites," she said. "I was six years old and singing with my mother at our county fair in Jackson, Tennessee. Your Grandmother Julia had an extraordinary voice. During Sunday morning service, she had people so moved they would either cry or jump in the aisles filled with joy."

Mama's eyes suddenly took on a faraway look. "People always told me I had the talent to be a gospel singer just like her. But when I was ten, mother passed away. And when she did, my dream of being a singer was buried right along with her. I felt so devastated, lonely, and empty. I just couldn't sing. Then Ada asked Papa to let me come live with her in Kentucky. With Ada's love and encouragement, I played the piano and started singing in the choir. With her kind ways and music, Ada helped me heal some of my pain of losing our mother. That's one of the reasons I sent you to spend the summer with her when Daddy and I separated."

Mama then pointed to another picture, her eyes brightening. "Here I am on my high school cheerleading squad," she said.

I studied the picture. I could hardly believe this young girl was Mama.

"I was just 19," Mama said. "After I finished high school I attended the local business college. That's where I met your handsome father and fell in love."

Silence filled the room. It had been a long time since I heard Mama express such loving words about Daddy.

Closing the metal box, she turned to me. "Sweetheart, every single day of my life, I face frustration and uncertainty. But that's okay as long as it doesn't lead to ignoring your dreams. I know this now more than ever. It took a long time, but I finally grew to appreciate your father's wish to write books. That was his dream and I regret standing in his way. Maybe that's why it's so important to me that you don't give up on your dream."

"Mama, what is your dream?" I said.

A half smile played on Mama's lips. "Well, my dream has already come true. I've always wanted to be a mother. I am so grateful to God for giving me the four of you. I know our life is hard but we'll always have each other. Papa Dennis would tell me after my mother died: 'in each life a little rain must fall.' But I want you to know that your life won't always be filled with rain. The sun will also come out. That's my promise to you."

Listening to Mama, I wondered, where she found her strength. More than a little rain had fallen into her life. In fact, it had been one full of terrible storms, including the most recent one—her daily battle with Multiple Sclerosis. She could have easily smothered the cruelties life had given her with alcohol or drugs. Instead she supported herself with her love for us and God. You might just say Mama's cane was love.

I really had no choice. I had to submit my application.

I couldn't be another line on Mama's long list of disappointments.

***

On the day of the audition, I woke up anxious and nervous. After dressing in the black skirt and white blouse Mama had purchased for the occasion, I quickly downed Mama's molasses drenched biscuits which sat like stones in my stomach. After kissing her good bye, I boarded the first of several buses that would take me to the audition.

The bus ride went without incident and I arrived early. I checked in at the registration desk and was escorted into a secluded hallway to wait. With sweaty hands, I practiced.

Once on stage, I tried to compose myself, taking in deep breaths through my nose and pushing out the tension through my mouth. I straightened my shoulders in an upright posture and smiled as I'd been taught. The judges sat at the table, their heads lowered. I hesitated, holding my violin and bow, awaiting the signal to begin.

In unison they raised their heads, puzzled.

A single voice boomed from the table. "Young lady we are on a schedule. What are you waiting for?"

I tucked my violin beneath my chin and pushed up my shoulder to hold it in place. My shoulders felt heavy as concrete. Perspiration began creeping along my frazzled hairline.

This terrible tension lessened a little as I played, but not much. In fact, I knew my first selection lacked the love I felt for the music. I wanted to stop playing the violin and start feeling the music.

At the end of my first piece, I watched the judges scribbling in their notepads. Without looking up, one of them said, "Please play your next piece."

I retuned my strings and again, shut my eyes. This time, I saw Mama in my mind, her body free of her steel wheels. Slowly I began to feel her presence. "This is for you, Mama," I repeated silently before I drew my bow.

When I'd finished my selection, I opened my eyes and looked towards the judge's table.

I waited, expecting some level of comment about my performance. But other than informing me that the results would be mailed, no other comments came.

There was nothing left to do but return home. After packing up my instrument, I ran to the bus wanting to get away from this foreign place as fast as possible.

As the bus headed home, I replayed the audition in my mind. Maybe I should not have closed my eyes when I played. Maybe the judges had felt shut out. Maybe Sister Jerome and Sister Leon Marie had led me down the wrong path. A million maybes, all pointing in one direction. I had failed.

When I reached home, Mama was sitting in her wheelchair near the tattered screen door. She rolled backwards, clearing the way for me.

As always, Mama had a lot of questions.

"Who were the judges? What did they say about your performance? What did the room look like? Did you meet any of the other girls?"

"Mama, I don't think they liked me, or my music!" I cried, flinging myself across the couch.

After a long moment, Mama beckoned for me to come and sit at her feet. She cupped my face in her hand and looked into my eyes. "Yolande, do you feel your performance was the best you could offer for this audition?"

"Yes. It was my best."

Mama's eyes held on to mine. "Then don't second guess your efforts. Regardless of the outcome, you practiced additional hours to prepare for this challenge. That's all that matters. Throughout your life there will be people who are less talented than you. But they will succeed because they refuse to accept failure. All you can do is give every experience your best. Stay focused. Stay positive. And let your angels do the rest. And now I have a favor to ask. Do you think you could play your selections again for me?"

I hardly felt like playing, but I couldn't refuse Mama. So I got out my violin. This time, I didn't close my eyes.

When I'd finished, the sun was slipping down, sending its tangerine light through the window, drenching the walls and floors. It glanced off Mama's steel wheels and braces and stained her skin a satiny gold. For one instant, it seemed everything in the room—Mama's figure, her steel wheels, the walls and the floor, and my violin's glossy wood were all wrapped up together, glowing in perfect harmony. I don't think I'd ever seen anything more beautiful.

"Come, sit with me," Mama said, dabbing at her tears with her faded apron. I knelt at her feet, circling her frail legs with my arms.

"This has been such a wonderful day. Let's pray."

Well truthfully, I'd stopped trying to pray like Mama long ago. Instead, I made lists in my head of all the things that made me happy. Not things like peach pie and skating shoes and crisp new blouses—though those were nice enough—but things that made me *really* happy. The kind of happy that's hard to describe. So as Mama's soft voice sounded above me, I began making my list.

First, I thought of my violin, a magical instrument that took me away from the ugliness and hurt around me.

The Lord is my shepherd; I shall not want...

I thought of Daddy. Even though he wasn't around much, I knew I was lucky to have a father who dreamed big and loved me. A father who'd read to me and wrote poems.

He maketh me to lie down in green pastures: he leadeth me beside the still waters. He restoreth my soul: he leadeth me in the paths of righteousness for his name's sake ...

I thought of my sister Jessica, and brothers, Greg and Kevin, and how lucky I was to have them. I knew we'd always be together, no matter what happened.

Yea, though I walk through the valley of the shadow of death, I will fear no evil: for thou art with me; they rod and thy staff they comfort me...

Inside my head, I saw the faces of Aunt Ada, Aunt Clara, Aunt Becky, Aunt Jack, Aunt Emma and other women who tried to help me. And I thought of Sister Jerome, Sister Leon Marie, Mr. Johnson, and Father Peete who'd believed in my music and had given me the courage to go beyond my neighborhood. And for a tiny second...a really tiny second... I even thought about Mother Superior.

Thou prepares a table before me in the presence of mine enemies; thou anointest my head with oil; my cup runneth over...

But most of all, I thought of Mama—the angel who was always with me, helping me in every way a mother could help a daughter.

Surely goodness and mercy shall follow me all the days of my life: and I will dwell in the house of the Lord forever.

When Mama finished her psalm, something that had felt closed inside me began to open. I really didn't understand what was happening, but I knew I would never be the same. It seemed like Mama's God had finally slipped into me because for the first time I felt my life had really changed. The miracle I'd longed for ever since I could remember had finally happened.

I was no longer a cursed child.

Discussion Questions

1. What does it mean to be 'cursed'? Why do you think the author felt cursed as a young girl?

2. Have you ever felt like a cursed child? Can you describe what or who made you feel this way? What or who helped you overcome these feelings?

3. During the story, we learn about a man named Jim Crow. Who was Jim Crow and what were Jim Crow laws? How did these laws affect the author and her family?

4. Why was Aunt Ada such an important role model for the author? Can you list someone who has helped or inspired you during difficult times? What did this person do?

5. What was the author's relationship to her parents as a young girl? What role did they play in her life?

6. Who were the villains in the story? Who were the heroes/heroines?

7. How did the difficult characters help the author grow?

8. The author often uses her mother's quotes in her story. How would you explain, "It's not *what* you go through but *how* you go through it."

9. Color plays a symbolic role in the story. How does the author use color to communicate ideas?

10. Why was the violin so important to the author?

11. List all the different gifts the author receives. Which three do you think were most important?

12. How does the end of the story relate to the book's title?

About the Author

Yolande Spears is Vice President of Education and Community Relations at The Bushnell Center for the Performing Arts, Connecticut's premiere performance venue for Broadway theatre, music, dance, children's theatre, and special events. As Vice President of Education, she co-created the Bushnell's award winning PARTNERS program. The program, which provides arts opportunities for students of all ages, is the recipient of numerous awards, among them a prestigious Dawson Award. The PARTNERS program has also received recognition for its outstanding work from The National Endowment for the Arts, the US Department of Education, the Connecticut Quality Innovative Award, and the Connecticut Department of Education. Additionally, PARTNERS was one of several organizations profiled in the Dana Foundation's 2003 publication, *Acts of Achievement.*

In her role as Vice President of Community Relations, Yolande has developed numerous family literacy and enrichment programs. In recognition of this work, The Broadway League selected The Bushnell as the first site to implement its *Family First Nights* program. This national initiative was designed to make Broadway programming accessible and more affordable for underserved families.

Along with her administrative leadership, Yolande has been a guest speaker at organizations throughout the United States, Canada, and in China. She's appeared at the National Endowment for the Arts, Music Theatre International, The Broadway League, the American Association of University Women, Harvard's Graduate School/Arts Education, the US Dept. of Education at Hoffstra University, Toronto Conservatory of Music, Beijing International Cultural & Creative Industry Expo, the Veteran Feminists of America, the Yale Goldman Sachs/National Business Plan Competition, the New England Conference for Gifted and Talented, and the Shanghai International Arts Festival, to mention a few.

In August 2005, Plays for Living commissioned her to write two short plays for a corporate client. Subsequently, her short story, "Buttered Biscuits" was published in the bestselling motivational series, *Wake Up & Live the Life You Love.*

Acknowledgements

I offer my deepest gratitude to the following friends and colleagues for the invaluable insights and incredible support they gave during the writing of this book: Margaret Wolfson, Maurice Hines, Jr., Archbishop LeRoy Bailey, Jr., Lois Lanning, Bruce Douglas, Sally M. Reis, Angela Curry, Zita Christian, Anne Douglas, and Reverend Dr. Shelley D. Best.

I am also indebted to my loving and much loved family: Amir, Rachel, Lanze, Greg, Kevin, Jessica, Etta, Jaime, Ayanna, Nettie, April, Lena, Theresa, Jean, and Angela, as well as all of my nephews, nieces, cousins, aunts, uncles, step children, god children, and the entire Williamson family.

My heartfelt thanks goes out to those who've played key roles in my professional life at Travelers Insurance Company, the Aetna, The Bushnell Center for the Performing Arts and other organizations. These are Michael Giuffrida, William Weiler, Doreen Spadorcia, William Davenport, Marlene Ibsen, Kevin Nicholson, Marilda Gándara, Linda Kelly, James Anderson, John Motley, The Bushnell's Board of Trustees and Overseers, David Fay, Ronna Reynolds, Elizabeth Ray, Kat Niedmann, Scott Galbraith, Michael Fresher, Brenda Dranoff Lopez, Dawn Petersen Jones, Mitchell Korn, Douglas Herbert, Gwen Smith Iloani, Theresa Hopkins-Staten, Douglas Evans, Deidre Tavera, Sonja Larkin Thorne, Felicity Harley, Terri Trotter, Princess Smith Sally, Shirley Cowles, Mary Kramer, Stacy Valentine, Polly Macpherson, Amy Ben-Kiki, Linda Regulbuto, Catherine Orzel, Jane Hartan, George Register,

Leslie Lerner, Virginia Bell, Robert Patricelli, Margaret Patricelli, Al Garcia, Kathy Matchett, Edmund Glazer, Jigang Zhang, Michael Sivo, Peter Simon, Donn Weinholtz, Jane Polin, Anne Witkavitch, Shenglai Chen, Michael Sullivan, Jr., Gigi Antoni, Raymond Arroyo, Dollie McLean, Judith Lisi, Rene Rodriguez, Chuck Metzgar, Shawn He Yuxun, Douglas Pick, Wendy Leigh, David Greer, Ana Sanchez Adorno, Anna Chen, Jatin Desai, Sandy Feng, Kiki Melendez, Morenga Hunt, Olivia White, Tara Schoen Fishman, Carlos Almonte, Pastor LeRoy Bailey, lll, Eric Coleman, Brad Davis, Frankie Goldfarb, Bob Goldfarb, Lena Fisher Butler, Curtis D. Robinson, Yvonne Davis, Joe Pannone, Scott Shuler, Kelvin Roldan, Janice Reynolds, Rod Reynolds, Dandanh He, Pam White, Ada Miranda, Yo Yo Yao, Megan Fitzgerald, Venton Forbes, Mari Rodriguez, Billie Scruse, Emilie Haifeng Wang, Charles Frazier, the faculty of Fontbonne University, The Bushnell's talented staff, PRIMER Group Members, and the Broadway League's Education Committee.

I also wish to thank the school administrators and teachers in Hartford, West Hartford, Plainville, Torrington, Bloomfield, East Hartford, New Britain, Farmington, Manchester, Bristol, Simsbury, and the many districts in the Capitol Region Education Council of Connecticut whose generous efforts enabled their students to experience the life-altering power of the arts through The Bushnell's PARTNERS program. I am especially grateful to Pat Moran, Robert Henry, Stacey McCann, Bruce Douglas, Kathy Grieder, Peg Beecher, Lois Lanning, Nancy Eastlake, Kathy Binkowski, June Bernabucci, Linda Van Wagenen, Sally M. Reis, Joseph Renzulli, Jackie Hardy, James Thompson, Percalee Morris, Peter Roach, Alice Davis, John Freeman, Shelley Mayfield, Marta Bentham, Delores Pertillar, Miriam Morales Taylor, David Sklarz, Kathy Gervais, Delores Bolton, Bessie Speers, Matt Fitzsimons, Wendy Allerton, Desi Nesmith, Pamela Totten-Alvarado, Dwight Fleming, Delia Bello-

Davila, Lynn Logoyke, Allison Douglas, Cathy Frayler, Dorothy Johnson, Norma Mailloux, Suzanne Greenbacker, Denise Gallucci, Jill Naraine, Sheilda Garrison, Joe Olzacki, Kathy Peete, Christina Kishimoto, Jean Purcell, Kris Berman, Angela Thomas, Anne Marie Mancini, Ruth Lyons, Herb Sheppard, Mary Kilray, and Haig Shahverdian.

The Bushnell's PARTNERS program couldn't function without its roster of multitalented artists. Among them are these master teaching and presenting artists; Andre Keitt, Margaret Wolfson, Carlos Hernández Chávez, Bessy Reyna, Cheryl Smith, Gene Bozzi, Dena Engelhardt, Joanne Scattergood, Lynn Hoffman, Elizabeth Thomas, Eugene Friesen, June Podagrosi, Motiko Dworkin, Ayanna Spears, Faithlyn Johnson, Sharon Dante, June Archer, Luis Cotto, Dan Butterworth, Pit Pinegar, Pam Nomura, Trent Artebery, Joseph Young, Jay Whitsett, Terryl Daluz, Keith Hughes, Mary Joy Moriarty, Maureen O'Brien, Deb Cowles, Victor Luna, Marcelina Sierras, Ray Gonzalez, Jolie Rocke Brown, Shenel Johns, Tim Moran, Rick Rozie, and Paula Chan Bing.

And of course this award winning program would not be possible without the ongoing support of individuals, corporations, and foundations. So on behalf of all the children, whose lives you've enriched beyond measure, I thank you.

Finally, I give my heartfelt thanks to Dr. Mark Josel, Dr. Zia Rahman, and Dr. Eric Van Rooy who helped me heal and survive. Without their talent and care, this book never would have been written.

Made in the USA
Middletown, DE
11 April 2018